the pleasure found in the pathless woods

Belinda Wood

BookLeaf Publishing

India | USA | UK

Presentation by *BookLeaf Publishing*

Web: www.bookleafpub.com

E-mail: info@bookleafpub.com

ISBN: 9789357446723

First edition 2022

ACKNOWLEDGEMENTS

For mum
Thank you for showing me that reality isn't
always real.
Love, always

aisle three

About the prowess of her,
theres a dictionary in the third aisle.
Section L-N, next to the audiophiles
When you open to page 555,
You'll find a love letter devoted to her
It'll read as followed;

There's romance in the air
with the notes teased lightly
from taut string straining against the touch
it dances from one note
to
the
next
It's a song, it collapses at the crescendo. upon
itself.

Sharp word, my sharper breath
I fall in love with your uncertain eyes
Oscillating from cloud to puddle.

But I'll stay contained
In the touch of a finger, asking to be unraveled

I am infatuated with the power that resides.

Find me in aisle 9.

Unimpressed, you'll snap it shut
And settle for a thriller by Sylvia Plath instead.

bone stock soup

why do i feel
so depleted
so empty
in this bone stock soup
eyes with grit and opening wide
falling down a gully (a spine)
unable to feel
the stable ground
all i want..
    i do not know
(be an island)

next

I saw it in his
eyes, in a twist of those
lips, a manufactured
smile and a trill in
his voice, he says
"Questioning what?"
It's in the warmth of
this touch, and that
feeling of flesh
on mine. He wraps
that comfort around my doubts
asks again,
"Questioning what?"
(but) I couldn't feel it in
the flames, my skin stopped burning
with his touch, and all this raging
fire behind my ribs, felt frigid
when he tugged me tighter
Scared to bruise his bruising heart
I said,
"I'm your conscious daydream,
I'm your awareness with a machete.
I'm a why at every point blank statement

And my thoughts,
they're the spiraling staircase
You climb for the milky way"

I untangled that comfort
undressed his quiet
contentment, I took his hand off
my flame, felt that heat
boil me alive
again.

in;manic

ill let the mood rise again
and wait as it sinks so low
there isn't much depth
felt in the waning of this moon.

ants

I think I have insects in my spine
Crawling with their pincers on my skin
and wings of paper battering my gut
Climbing the bones of my ribs,
and laying eggs in my throat
You gave me ants under the eye socket.
And I felt them pull through the kidney
I felt them pull and I thought,
This must be it
That stars in the eyes and
butterflies in the
belly kind of
kick.

I have a tendency to attach to air,
The further away they feel, the closer I feel to
nothing.

butter

Some days we melt with that buttery softness
    on   hot   steaming   bread
Other days we're stuck with the oil on old pans

The flow in our textures grinds my resolve
When late hour fingers trace their caress
And lace their secrets through mine
Creeping through the burn under my ribs
still, i feel those lips are mine

find gratitude(

(I didnt know i held this ocean within)
I leak a little bit more every day, but the ocean
 of these tears refuse to dry
And life is a balance of stretching rubber
When it's good, its white flames.
 The scent in the grass is spring-heaven,
and the composition of
light burning from a
star above - the encapsulating moment
held is ecstasy.
But goddess forgive, for when
it's worse than great, I forget every
ounce of gratitude. I have nothing to
be thankful for, because it's never
more than enough. I become a
sinking pit, taking the bleakness and
frowning at their praise.

The question that rests is this
Would I remove the bleakness at the expense of
ecstasy?

To tip the scale would be the take the empty
despair,
replace the extremities of ranges of something
surely inadequate
I'd feel comfortably okay
Or uncomfortably numb

the tuesdays with you

(how reckless it'd be
to consider you
when all i crave
is a hunger sated
from knowing a wizened me)

if our pathways were meant to cross,
i'd shoulder barge you, we're bound to meet.
every tuesday. before 11am. sour espresso on
my tongue.
(and if the old man on the broken love seat
at 2.30am in the middle of a west end love story
believes a soul mate is on their way
then who am i disagree with his belief)
 the man child (with a crypto account no doubt)
Thinks there's love on a square by square feed
(he dm's the ones he considers out of his league,
asks their favourite shade of pink) (its folly,
they're all out of his league)
This man tries to tell me the universe is empty
then asks me why i weep
(not soft and silent in his fake leather jacket, but
banshee bawling tears in a crowd)
(the old man watches and thinks it's his first or

second life)
if all of these fate laden crossovers stayed
coincidences
and we were meant to meet
then why haven't we met
every tuesday
with salty eyes
and dreaded hair
we never did. Maybe soulmates don't exist.

the fear

The curve rounded its way down, (as curves do
best)
Spiraling towards sharp edges, and things best
left unetched
(dont etch your initials in the trunk of a tree)
I hid inside more than I liked to admit
I strayed away more than I wandered near
Fear was a feeling in my gut, and a story that
pursed these lips.
Cut the amygdala. Control your fate.

the weird

there's tension with the old man at the butcher
who follows me around the aisles
and stands between my father and i
and there's tension with the stranger lifting
weights
who looks close to crushing my softness with
callous hands
and there was tension between the friend who
loops so easily in
its funny how we all fall into place.
and it feels like one of those moments
that falling into place kind of moment.

the hope

My mother smothered her today.
In warm oil dripping from her dropping skin,
And fingers soft on that throat.
I pulled her under the day before,
With the water, I gathered
In the well by his yard.
I'll drown her again tomorrow.

We found it in a jar under my grandmothers'
house
and the oil, I traced a flower on her heart
He stole the fear from fearful eyes
and she saw, wide open, for the first time.

All that tar stuck in her lungs
we came in groups and extracted it clear.
And her thoughts, i kissed sweetly in farewell
then father stabbed her stumbling hesitation
threw a white flag on the battlefield and
mouthed
be still.

there wasn't a gasp
or a cry for breath
she surrendered to the death.
to live again.

turning twenty-two

dispassionately on the outs of love
 (and out of things to talk about)
it's that high brow cringe (disgust)
and the thankful message from her on your
screen
(do you remember how uncomfortable the moon
made us feel)

Golden curls and light dancing on the skin.
Hold you so close you fly away
Hand over heart, I sing
I'm in, I'm in

you delicately crumbled
with each step I took within.

(hands that held it together
 hold her instead
so i hold myself
and orgasm instead)

isn't it curious how much
an ending feels like an ending

•

can you help me clean the bathroom
I'm not sure where to start
or where to stop
but you can start there
  and i will go stay here
because
    I'm only failing
with human choices,
  letting the dishes pile high around me
laying in the grass
 outside a tattered house
in the weeds that hide…
god, whats lying behind the pathless path

the secret.

I want to be found out
(but I dont want to be the unliked)
I leave receipts on tables and my email lays open
(the quicker im found out the quicker i can
sleep)
There's a shade of lipstick i never owned
Its on the collar of his shirt. he calls her crazy
for noticing.
When my darling comes home, i hide the lace
and turn down the fire
He's asked me about my day and i tell him he
never cares so why ever ask.
And when he comes to hold me from behind -
im making his sons dinner.
I stay so still and wait for the onslaught to be
over.
Then i hide on the porch outside and tell him its
me, it's fine.
Go to bed, i'll follow soon. You too.

repeat after me.

Repeat after me.

I am whole
I am worthy of love
and I am capable to give it
infinite in form, i am encompassing all.

you are an energy.
tantalisingly real,
steeping your tea and tapping your pigeon-toe
feet
electric in your execution, you touch it
it's magnifique.
a wildling
with calloused feet,
(be a wolf sneering at crisp white sheets)

but there's shadows
creeping through your mind
tendrils of doubt, and that wicked shame.
a darker side with a ringing voice,
turns the tea bitter.
it's endeavoured mission; the undoing of you

it works each hour-long-second to discredit, then
devalue
and snarks *chuck it out and embarras us again!*

the glowing capacity, and everything it entails
your beauty is not measured
against the light of another
it would be unjust to pick just one
when they are the still full moon
and you're the goliath rising sun

your truest mask is joy. Be true.

the memory.

~when did it fall apart?
It fell to pieces on so many days
I lost count of them along the way
But if I had to pick a moment
So clear in my mind, it might be
The day I cut my hair when he asked
He said he liked that urban vibe
It was the times I kept myself quiet
Because he liked to be loud
I tried to dream with him
But did it so clumsily
That it turned to rage and a door in my face
One morning I asked him to escape with me
To be a little daring, *let's run away*
But a crushed hope sounded like *how dare you*
Maybe that was when I knew I couldn't be with
a him
That kept eyes staring below the ceiling
How much I learned to hate
A gaze drawn low, fearing fate
And I could deal with his anxiety
His stress loaded onto mine
I could carry him on these shoulders

how strong they are
And I could hold him in these hands
Soft and small, but I could keep it held
But it was the static I couldn't take
I could love a wounded soldier
But not a lover with a wish to die
I'll find a medic I said
There's nothing wrong with a bit of disease
Let it bleed he mumbled at my breaking heart

[No title].

when words of love
are poured into a shadow
do they sweeten like honey
or turn bitter with the brew

the regret

I wrote to you
Letter after stupid letter
I poured my heart into a diary
Ripped the pages and burnt them
The ash became steaming piles of your bullshit.

you were rude to the goddamn waiter
are the words I should have written
in the journal dedicated to the romanticization of
you
but i gushed about the spoken poetry you played
and the raw vegetables you served

the waiter offered you the menu
you didn't look him in the face
when you told him the table was shit
and the wine, you knew nothing about the wine.

(i thought you remembered him, you acted as though
 he was the lover your ex fucked on the first
date)

the thing is, I went vegan for it, whatever it was

Love, or lust, or karmic bullshit kicking me back
(was I bitch in a past life?)
I ate the bullshit with a spoon and sauce, called
it gourmet dessert.
What are you thinking
....you wouldnt want to know
Try me. Those walls are high, why can't I get in?

the discovery

And with a curiosity, I stared at her
I felt her neck tilt and watched that stare turn
dark
She had her knee propped against the wall, her
left leg folded beneath
An inky hint of ocean on an ankle
And the jewellery in her face almost tinkled
How wonderous this creature was, I thought
How beautifully she sits
With elegance in her fingers
But theres a tense set to her shoulders
Pushed back and neck aiming high
Her lips in a practiced pout
Does she know
How curious
she is
How wild
the heart ticks
And how struck I am
By the feel of her touch
and the feel of me

the hint

he took the whiskey
Straight bourbon on the rocks
he spoke with rolling tongues
    i rescued cats,
Speederlings,
Snakes y saved the rrats

he didnt speak to my eyes
Or my mouth
He spoke to my chest
And the piercing
Like all of the rest

My obsession is to reject
Then pine
And when they are too close
I walk a little
And let them wonder if
I'll ever
look
back

Hello, you.

It sprung back.
There was a thought that it disappeared
To evaporate into the nothing of nothing
And the angle of a perspective that shifted
Ever   so   slightly
That if i'm being honest,
I wondered if it ever existed.

Storm at midnight, it flashed lightning on my
walls
And the longer i stay contained
The tighter the clench in my jaw.
What is to be made of   you

today i disappear
I'm invisible in a crowd
and there's a pathless step through this town
the eyes looking past the reality of today

the only real is the taste on the tongue
and the guttural
heavy
breathing from these lungs

I'm a stranger on the streets, I stumble on the
walk home
I'm a mannequin in the sheep's clothing,
hanging too tight, too loose
threads give and peel
 back from their shape.
curving through the force
full of nature (curving, curving down as curves
do best)
Warming my blood with -

the conviction of you

(Next page)
pleasure; found